Rhythm and Rhyme

A READ WITH ME BOOK

Senior Authors

Roger C. Farr

Dorothy S. Strickland

Authors

Richard F. Abrahamson ◆ Alma Flor Ada ◆ Barbara Bowen Coulter
Bernice E. Cullinan ◆ Margaret A. Gallego
W. Dorsey Hammond
Nancy Roser ◆ Junko Yokota ◆ Hallie Kay Yopp

Senior Consultant

Asa G. Hilliard III

Consultants

Lee Bennett Hopkins ◆ David A. Monti ◆ Rosalia Salinas

Harcourt Brace & Company

Orlando Atlanta Austin Boston San Francisco Chicago Dallas New York Toronto London

Requests for permission to make copies of any part of the work should be mailed to the following address: School Permissions, Harcourt Brace & Company, 6277 Sea Harbor Drive, Orlando, Florida 32887-6777.

HARCOURT BRACE and Quill Design is a registered trademark of Harcourt Brace & Company.

Portions of this work were published in previous editions.

Acknowledgments appear in the back of this work.

Printed in the United States of America

ISBN 0-15-310804-5

3 4 5 6 7 8 9 10   048   2000 99

Dear Reader,

You probably already know that books can be a lot of fun—you can meet new friends, visit new places, and learn new things. Now you will find that books can be even more fun if the words in them have **rhythm and rhyme!**

As you read the stories in this book, you'll want to grab a friend and clap, tap, chant, laugh, and share the stories over and over again. So come on—let's have fun!

Sincerely,

The Authors

The Authors

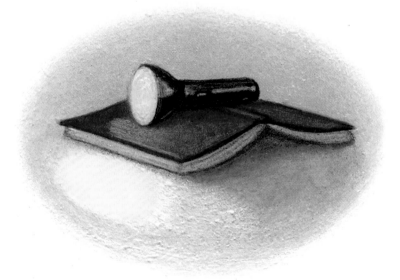

CONTENTS

Theme 1: When Friends Get Together

Theme 2: Clap Your Hands! Tap Your Toes!

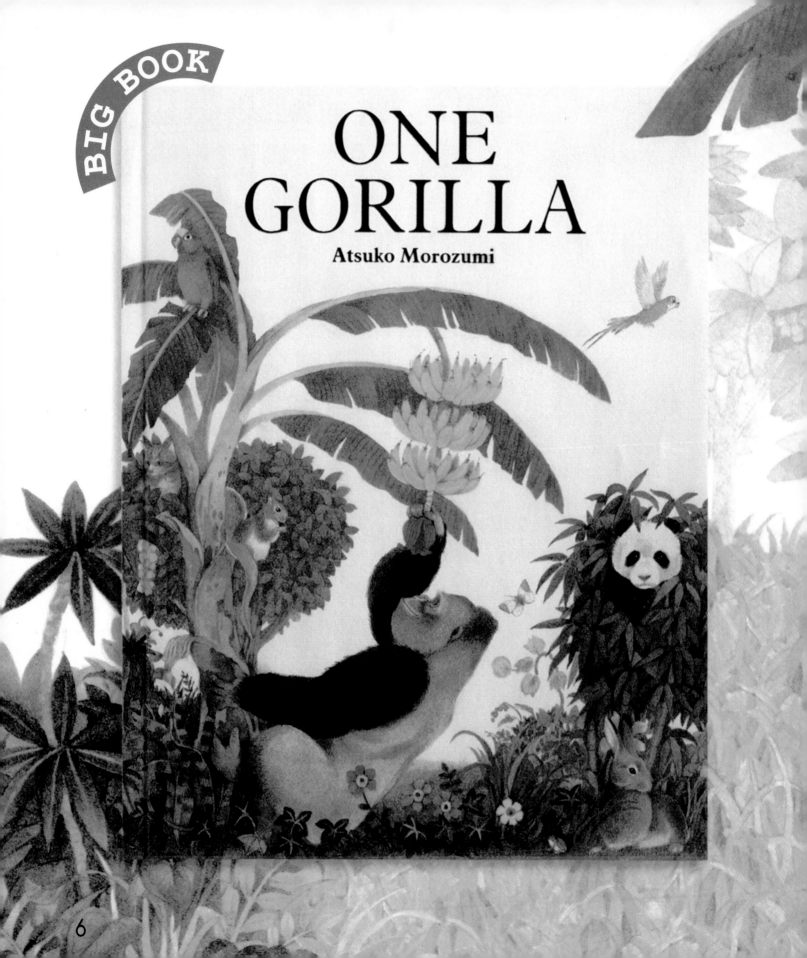

ONE
GORILLA

Atsuko Morozumi

7

Here is a list of things I love.
One gorilla.

9

Two butterflies among the flowers and one gorilla.

Three parakeets in my house
and one gorilla.

Four squirrels in the woods
and one gorilla.

Five pandas in the snow
and one gorilla.

17

18

Six rabbits in a field
and one gorilla.

19

Seven frogs by the fence
and one gorilla.

21

Eight fish in the sea
and one gorilla.

Nine birds among the leaves and one gorilla.

Ten cats in my garden
and one gorilla.

10 cats

9 birds

8 fish

7 frogs

6 rabbits

5 pandas

4 squirrels

3 parakeets

2 butterflies

But where is my gorilla?

Ah, there he is.

31

"PARDON?"

SAID THE GIRAFFE

by Colin West

BIG BOOK

"PARDON?"
SAID THE
GIRAFFE

Colin West

"What's it like up there?"
asked the frog
as he hopped on the ground.

"Pardon?"
said the
giraffe.

"What's it like up there?"
asked the frog
as he hopped on the lion.

"Pardon?" said the giraffe.

"What's it like up there?"
asked the frog
as he hopped on the hippo.

"Pardon?"
said the
giraffe.

"What's it like up there?"
asked the frog
as he hopped on the elephant.

"Pardon?"
said the giraffe.

"What's it like up there?"
asked the frog
as he hopped on the giraffe.

"It's nice up here, thank you,"
said the giraffe,
"but you're tickling my nose
and I think I'm going to . . ."

44

"Oooooops!"
said the frog.

"What's it like down there?"
asked the giraffe.

"Pardon?"
said the frog.

ARE YOU THERE, BEAR?

by Ron Maris

reillustrated by Lori Lohstoeter

My room is dark and quiet.
Are you there, Bear?
Under my bed?

52

That's not a bear.
Come out, Donkey!

In my cupboard?

That's not a bear.
Come out,
Little Doll!

Up here, in my box?

That's not a bear.
Go back, Jack!

63

Over here, in my basket?

That's not a bear.
Come out, Raggety!

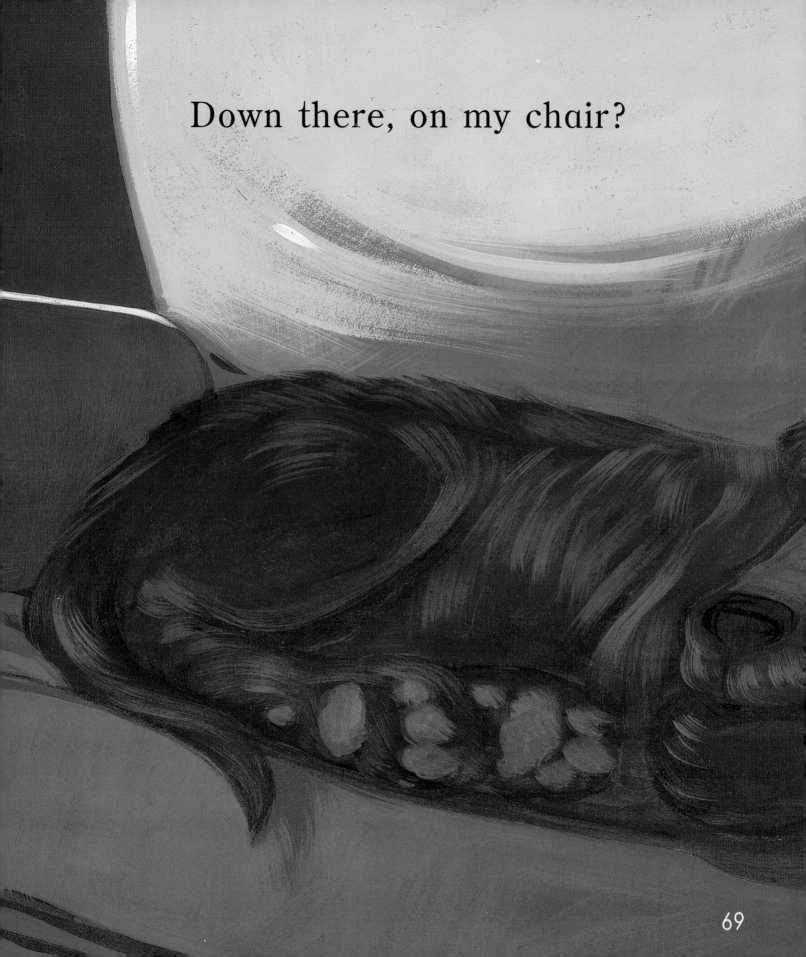

Down there, on my chair?

That's not a bear.
Come out, Spike!

71

What is that?

Who is there,
beside my chair?

Bear is there! With a book . . .

. . . tell us a story, Bear.

Adapted by Bill Martin Jr.

Fire! Fire! Said Mrs. McGuire

Illustrated by Nathan Jarvis

"Fire! Fire!" said Mrs. McGuire.

"Where? Where?" said Mrs. Bear.

"Down town!" said Mrs. Brown.

"What floor?" said Mrs. Moore.

"Near the top!" said Mrs. Kopp.

"What a pity!" said Mrs. Kitty.

"Help! Help!" said Mrs. Kelp.

"Here I come!" said Mrs. Plumb.

"Water! Water!" said Mrs. Votter.

"Get out of my way!" said Mrs. Lei.

"Let me see!" said Mrs. Chi.

"Break down the door!" said Mrs. Orr.

"Well, I declare!" said Mrs. Wear.

"Oh help us and save us!"
said Mrs. Davis
as she fell down the stairs
with a sack of potatoes.

Acknowledgments
For permission to reprint copyrighted material, grateful acknowledgment is made to the following sources:
Farrar, Straus & Giroux, Inc.: One Gorilla: A Counting Book by Atsuko Morozumi. Text copyright © 1990 by Mathew Price; illustrations copyright © 1990 by Atsuko Morozumi.
Greenwillow Books, a division of William Morrow & Company, Inc.: Are you there, Bear? by Ron Maris. Text copyright © 1984 by Ron Maris.
Harcourt Brace & Company: Fire! Fire! Said Mrs. McGuire by Bill Martin Jr. Text copyright © 1970 by Harcourt Brace & Company.
Walker Books Ltd., London: "Pardon?" Said the Giraffe by Colin West. Copyright © 1986 by Colin West.

Illustration Credits
Mary Jane Begin, Cover art; Nathan Jarvis, 4-5; Atsuko Morozumi, 8-31; Colin West, 32-49; Lori Lohstoeter, 50-79; Nathan Jarvis, 80-95

Printed in the United States of America
ISBN 0-15-310804-5